Contents

THIS IS THE **BLUR** QUIZBOOK

The Quizbook is intended to take you through the entire career o
Blur (All information correct at time of writing November 2024)

It starts from the early beginnings in rough chronology through t
the present day.

The book includes sections of multiple-choice questions. In betwee
the multiple-choice questions there will be a lyrics quiz based on eac
of the Blur albums

There will also be questions relating to recordings the band member
made away from Blur

Each section can be cross referenced against the answers provide
towards the end of the book.

Grab a drink, a pencil, put on some Blur and enjoy the quizbook – o
take it to your friends and fill out together – quiz your best mate wh
claims to know everything about Blur and see how much they trul
know.

Most of all – enjoy the journey of this band from small intimate gig
to world tours.

B DEMURE

Blur Quizbook

Early Days

1. Which additional instrument did Graham play on early Demos written by Damon?

   a) Trombone ☐

   b) Trumpet ☐

   c) Clarinet ☐

   d) Saxophone ☐

2. What was the name of the earliest iteration of the band featuring Damon, Graham and Dave? It was changed shortly afterwards with the arrival of Alex

   a) Cruise ☐

   b) Sharpie ☐

   c) Circus ☐

   d) Parallel ☐

3. What was the name of the band from 1988-1990 before they settled on Blur?

    a) Claymore ☐

    b) Timor ☐

    c) Gilmour ☐

    d) Seymour ☐

4. At which London college did Damon, Alex and Graham all study?

    a) Blacksmiths ☐

    b) Oldsmiths ☐

    c) Goldsmiths ☐

    d) Silversmiths ☐

5. In 1988 the band made their first live appearance in the goods shed of which museum?

    a) Colchester Castle ☐

    b) Hollytrees Museum ☐

    c) St Johns Abbey ☐

    d) East Anglian Railway ☐

6. Which record label signed the band in 1990 as the band were rechristened to Blur?

    a) Grub Records ☐

    b) Food Records ☐

    c) Time Records ☐

    d) Second Records ☐

7. In February 1990 the band played their first gig as Blur in which London venue?

    a) Brixton Academy ☐

    b) The Dublin Castle ☐

    c) The Lexington ☐

    d) The Good Ship ☐

8. Between March and July 1990 Blur toured Britain in support of which band?

    a) The Alarm ☐

    b) The Folds ☐

    c) The Cramps ☐

    d) The Farm ☐

9. Blur made their first TV appearance in April 1991 performing "There's No Other Way" on which Saturday morning TV show?

    a) TV Mayhem ☐

    b) Eggs 'n' Baker ☐

    c) Wide Awake Club ☐

    d) The Chart Show ☐

10. Blur played their first gig outside of the UK and Ireland in February 1991 in which Dutch city?

    a) Amsterdam ☐

    b) Groningen ☐

    c) Rotterdam ☐

    d) Breda ☐

(ANSWERS CAN BE FOUND ON PAGE 73)

SECTION TWO

Leisure Era

1. What is the opening track of the album? It was also the band's debut single released in October 1991

   a) Slow Down ☐

   b) Bang ☐

   c) She's So High ☐

   d) Bad Day ☐

2. The cover photograph of the album features a lady with what headwear?

   a) A Headscarf ☐

   b) A Nurses Hat ☐

   c) A Bandana ☐

   d) Bathing Hat ☐

3. What number did the album peak at in the UK album chart?

    a) 2 ☐

    b) 7 ☐

    c) 10 ☐

    d) 14 ☐

4. Which album track was included on the Trainspotting film soundtrack?

    a) Sing ☐

    b) Fool ☐

    c) High Cool ☐

    d) Repetition ☐

5. In a 1991 interview which American singer stated that "There's No Other Way" was his favourite British song of the year?

    a) Michael Stipe ☐

    b) Michael Jackson ☐

    c) Bruce Springsteen ☐

    d) Kurt Cobain ☐

6. What is featured inching through the grass at the opening of the video for "There's No Other Way"?

    a) A Butterfly ☐

    b) A Worm ☐

    c) A Snake ☐

    d) A Beetle ☐

7. What board game are the band playing in the "Bang" video?

    a) Scrabble ☐

    b) Monopoly ☐

    c) Trivial Pursuit ☐

    d) Operation ☐

8. Complete the title of this album track – "Wear Me _____"

    a) Down ☐

    b) Out ☐

    c) Now ☐

    d) Dress ☐

9. Working alongside the band who produced the majority of the songs on the album?

    a) Stephen Street ☐

    b) Charles Street ☐

    c) Michael Street ☐

    d) Peter Street ☐

10. In 1992 Blur released a non-album single - what was it titled?

    a) Popworld ☐

    b) Popout ☐

    c) Popscene ☐

    d) Popshow ☐

(ANSWERS CAN BE FOUND ON PAGE 74)

SECTION THREE

Modern Life is Rubbish Era

1. Prior to the release of the album Blur went on a tour to the United States alongside the "Jesus and Mary Chain" amongst others - what was the tour entitled?

    a) Roundabout Tour ☐

    b) Rollercoaster Tour ☐

    c) Waltzer Tour ☐

    d) Tightrope Tour ☐

2. Blurs American label was dissatisfied after being sent the finished tapes of the album - they demanded that the album should be re-recorded and produced by which US producer? (Blur refused)

    a) Phil Spector ☐

    b) Tony Visconti ☐

    c) Butch Vig ☐

    d) Rick Rubin ☐

3. What was the working title of the album? They changed it to "Modern Life is Rubbish" after seeing it written in graffiti on a wall on Bayswater Road

    a) Away from Today ☐

    b) Into the Swarm ☐

    c) Pantheon Rising ☐

    d) Britain Vs America ☐

4. What features on the front cover of the standard edition of the album?

    a) A Steam Train ☐

    b) A Motor Car ☐

    c) A Moped ☐

    d) A Yacht ☐

5. What is the title of the albums opening track?

    a) Advert ☐

    b) Blue Jeans ☐

    c) Miss America ☐

    d) For Tomorrow ☐

6. Complete the title of this album track –
"Pressure on _____"

    a) James ☐

    b) Julian ☐

    c) Jeeves ☐

    d) Jeremy ☐

7. What was the name of the US label that
released the album?

    a) AMS ☐

    b) PBS ☐

    c) LUS ☐

    d) SBK ☐

8. Which Rod Stewart song was covered and
released on the B-side of the 7" single release of
"Chemical World"?

    a) Forever Young ☐

    b) Sailing ☐

    c) Maggie May ☐

    d) Tonight's the Night ☐

9. What foodstuff appears on the cover of the single "Sunday Sunday"?

   a) A Burger ☐

   b) Fries ☐

   c) A Hot Dog ☐

   d) Chicken Wings ☐

10. In 1993 which song by The Who did Blur cover for a special "Who Covers Who?" Compilation covers album?

   a) My Generation ☐

   b) Behind Blue Eyes ☐

   c) Who Are You ☐

   d) Substitute ☐

(ANSWERS CAN BE FOUND ON PAGE 75)

SECTION FOUR

Complete the Leisure and Modern Life is Rubbish Lyric

(Five songs from each album)

1. She's so high, I want to _____ all over her

2. Waiting for an underground train to _____ underneath my feet

3. Do you _____ anyone you ever loved? Love

4. You're making me run, when I don't wanna _____

5. But couldn't you try to _____ a fool one more time?

6. But we're lost on the _____, and so we hold each other tightly

7. I wash with new soap behind the _____, helps keep down the laundry

8. The _____ says that she's out in a week, what a shame, she was just getting comfy

9. He fought for us in two world wars, says the _____ he knew is now no more

10. Speaking drivel, can it get confused with heavy _____

(ANSWERS CAN BE FOUND ON PAGE 76)

SECTION FIVE

Alex in Profile

1. What is Alex's full birth name?

    a) Peter Alexander James ☐

    b) James Alexander Stephens ☐

    c) Steven Alexander James ☐

    d) Alexander Ian James ☐

2. Where was Alex born?

    a) Brighton ☐

    b) Blackpool ☐

    c) Birmingham ☐

    d) Bournemouth ☐

3. In 1980 on the day John Lennon was shot Alex was off from school with which illness?

    a) Laryngitis ☐

    b) Appendicitis ☐

    c) Chickenpox ☐

    d) Pneumonia ☐

4. Which band did Alex form alongside Keith Allen and Damien Hirst in 1998?

   a) The Meteors ☐

   b) Fat Les ☐

   c) New Order ☐

   d) Black Grape ☐

5. What type of farm does Alex run in Oxfordshire?

   a) Cheese Farm ☐

   b) Poultry Farm ☐

   c) Arable Farm ☐

   d) Organic Farm ☐

6. What was the title of Sophie Ellis-Bexter's debut album that James helped produce, has writing credits on - as well as providing bass guitar?

   a) Read My Lips ☐

   b) Make a Scene ☐

   c) Wanderlust ☐

   d) Familia ☐

7. What is the name of Alex's wife whom he married in 2003?

    a) Christine ☐

    b) Rhiannan ☐

    c) Claire ☐

    d) Sharon ☐

8. How many children does James have?

    a) Two ☐

    b) Three ☐

    c) Four ☐

    d) Five ☐

9. What is the name of Alex's show on Classic FM every Saturday night between 19:00-22:00?

    a) Alex James's Party Night ☐

    b) Alex James's Blurry Night ☐

    c) Alex James's Date Night ☐

    d) Alex James's Late Night ☐

10. Since 2012 what is the name of the food and music festival he has hosted on his farm?

    a) The Foodie Festival ☐

    b) Food and Booze Festival ☐

    c) Feast For Your Ears ☐

    d) The Big Feastival ☐

(ANSWERS CAN BE FOUND ON PAGE 77)

Parklife Era

1. What was the first track to be released from Parklife in March 1994?

    a) In the End ☐

    b) Girls & Boys ☐

    c) End of a Century ☐

    d) Parklife ☐

2. In what London studio was the album recorded?

    a) Maison Rouge ☐

    b) Maison Bleu ☐

    c) Maison Verde ☐

    d) Maison Rose ☐

3. What dogs feature on the front cover of the album?

    a) Greyhounds ☐

    b) Poodles ☐

    c) Bulldogs ☐

    d) Alsatians ☐

4. What was the working title of the album?

    a) Earth ☐

    b) Britain ☐

    c) England ☐

    d) London ☐

5. Which Quadrophenia star featured on title track "Parklife"?

    a) Paul Daniels ☐

    b) Phil Davis ☐

    c) Phil Daniels ☐

    d) Paul Davis ☐

6. All lyrics on the album are attributed to Damon with the exception of which Alex James penned track?

    a) Far Out ☐

    b) Tracy Jacks ☐

    c) London Loves ☐

    d) Clover Over Dover ☐

7. Lætitia Sadier provides vocals on "To the End" - with which band did she make her name?

    a) Broadcast ☐

    b) Super Furry Animals ☐

    c) Stereolab ☐

    d) Deerhunter ☐

8. "End of a Century" was the last single to be released from the album - the music video features a live performance at which London venue?

    a) Wembley Arena ☐

    b) O2 Islington ☐

    c) Brixton Academy ☐

    d) Alexandra Palace ☐

9. Complete the title of this instrumental track from the album "The _____ Collector"

    a) Tax ☐

    b) Debt ☐

    c) Law ☐

    d) Love ☐

10. Which track from the album was released as a promotional single by the band in January 1995?

    a) This Is a Low ☐

    b) End of a Century ☐

    c) To the End ☐

    d) Jubilee ☐

(ANSWERS CAN BE FOUND ON PAGE 78)

The Great Escape Era

1. "Country House" was the first single to be released from the album - it became the band's first number one. Which Oasis single did it famously trump to grab the number one spot?

    a) Live Forever ☐

    b) Wonderwall ☐

    c) Some Might Say ☐

    d) Roll with It ☐

2. The "Country House" video was nominated for Best Video at the 1996 Brit Awards - who directed the video?

    a) Damien Hirst ☐

    b) Tracey Emin ☐

    c) Banksy ☐

    d) Anish Kapoor ☐

3. Complete the title of this album track "He Thought of _____"

    a) Her ☐

    b) Himself ☐

    c) Cars ☐

    d) Shapes ☐

4. Which politician provided narration on "Ernold Same"?

    a) Jack Straw ☐

    b) Ken Livingstone ☐

    c) Margaret Beckett ☐

    d) Alistair Darling ☐

5. Which film inspired the music video for "The Universal"?

    a) Animal Farm ☐

    b) Eyes Wide Shut ☐

    c) Full Metal Jacket ☐

    d) A Clockwork Orange ☐

6. "Stereotypes" was original planned to be the lead single from the album but "Country House" got a huge reaction when the band played a secret gig to debut the songs at which London venue?

   a) Dublin Castle ☐

   b) The Astoria ☐

   c) The 100 Club ☐

   d) Hope and Anchor ☐

7. The front cover of the album features which mode of transport?

   a) Bus ☐

   b) Train ☐

   c) Blimp ☐

   d) Speedboat ☐

8. Complete the title of this album track "Mr. Robinson's _____"

   a) Quandary ☐

   b) Quango ☐

   c) Quest ☐

   d) Question ☐

9. What was the fourth and final single to be released from the album?

    a) The Universal ☐

    b) Charmless Man ☐

    c) Stereotypes ☐

    d) Top Man ☐

10. What is the title of the final track on the album?

    a) Dan Abnormal ☐

    b) Globe Alone ☐

    c) Yuko and Hiro ☐

    d) Entertain Me ☐

(ANSWERS CAN BE FOUND ON PAGE 79)

SECTION EIGHT

Complete the Parklife and The Great Escape Lyric

(Five songs from each album)

1. Nothing is wasted, only reproduced, you get nasty _____

2. The mind gets dirty, as you get closer to _____

3. I get up when I want, except on _____ when I get rudely awakened by the dustmen

4. All those dirty words, they make us look so _____

5. Hit traffic on the Dogger Bank, up the _____ to find a Taxi rank

6. She's most accommodating when she's in her _____

7. Touched with his own mortality, he's reading Balzac and knocking back _____

8. He knows the swingers and their _____ says he can get in anywhere for free

9. No one here is alone, _____ in every home

10. All we want is to be happy, in our homes like happy _____

(ANSWERS CAN BE FOUND ON PAGE 80)

SECTION NINE

Graham in Profile

1. What is Grahams full name?

   a) Graham Ellis Coxon ☐

   b) Graham Leslie Coxon ☐

   c) Graham Sharp Coxon ☐

   d) Graham Charles Coxon ☐

2. Where was Graham born?

   a) Salzburg, Austria ☐

   b) Avignon, France ☐

   c) Rinteln, Germany ☐

   d) Pisa, Italy ☐

3. What football team does Graham support?

   a) Nottingham Forest ☐

   b) Leeds United ☐

   c) Stockport County ☐

   d) Derby County ☐

4. As a child which popular children's T.V show did Graham appear on twice?

    a) Blue Peter ☐

    b) Magpie ☐

    c) New Faces ☐

    d) Opportunity Knocks ☐

5. What did Graham study whilst at college?

    a) Chemistry ☐

    b) Biology ☐

    c) Music ☐

    d) Fine Arts ☐

6. What is the title of Grahams debut solo album released in 1998?

    a) The Sky is Too High ☐

    b) The Sun is Too Close ☐

    c) The Earth is Too Small ☐

    d) The Night is Too Short ☐

7. What member of Pink Floyd heavily influenced Graham?

    a) David Gilmour ☐

    b) Roger Waters ☐

    c) Syd Barrett ☐

    d) Nick Mason ☐

8. In 2005 Graham released a DVD entitled "Live at the _____" what?

    a) Nemesis ☐

    b) Zodiac ☐

    c) College ☐

    d) Union ☐

9. Graham plays guitar on the album "Grace/Wastelands" released in 2009 by which artist?

    a) Thom Yorke ☐

    b) Morrissey ☐

    c) Billy Bragg ☐

    d) Peter Doherty ☐

10. What is the title of Coxon's memoir published in October 2022?

    a) Verse, Chorus, Magic! ☐

    b) Verse, Chords, Verse! ☐

    c) Verse, Chorus, Monster! ☐

    d) Verse, Chorus, Repeat! ☐

(ANSWERS CAN BE FOUND ON PAGE 81)

Blur (Album) Era

1. What is the location featured on the front cover of the album?

    a) A Police Station ☐

    b) A Shopping Mall ☐

    c) A Library ☐

    d) A Hospital ☐

2. The recording of the album took place in London and which other European capital?

    a) Brussels ☐

    b) Reykjavik ☐

    c) Copenhagen ☐

    d) Amsterdam ☐

3. Which track from the album was Graham given solo lyric writing credit for?

    a) Look Inside America ☐

    b) Theme from Retro ☐

    c) Death of a Party ☐

    d) You're So Great ☐

4. What was the first single to be released from the album in January 1997?

    a) Song 2 ☐

    b) Beetlebum ☐

    c) On Yor Own ☐

    d) Strange News from Another Star ☐

5. Which song from the album featured on multiple FIFA video games notably FIFA: Road to World Cup 98?

    a) On Your Own ☐

    b) Theme from Retro ☐

    c) Beetlebum ☐

    d) Song 2 ☐

6. Complete the title of this album track
   "Chinese _____"

   a) Democracy ☐

   b) Bombs ☐

   c) Money ☐

   d) Hopes ☐

7. David Bowie and Brian Eno receive credit for
   which track due to similarities to two tracks
   from album "Lodger"?

   a) F.O.R ☐

   b) P.D.R ☐

   c) M.O.R ☐

   d) X.Y.Z ☐

8. "On Your Own" features in the soundtrack to
   which film released in 2000?

   a) Sexy Beast ☐

   b) Road Trip ☐

   c) Gladiator ☐

   d) The Beach ☐

9. Prior to the release of the album Blur released a live album entitled "Live at the Budokan" in which country was it recorded?

    a) Japan ☐

    b) China ☐

    c) Indonesia ☐

    d) Bulgaria ☐

10. What is the title of the final track on the album (excluding hidden tracks)?

    a) Essex Dogs ☐

    b) Essex Days ☐

    c) Essex Ways ☐

    d) Essex Plays ☐

(ANSWERS CAN BE FOUND ON PAGE 82)

13 Era

1. Prior to the release of "13" Blur released a remix/live compilation album - what was its title?

    a) Dancin' + Dreamin' ☐

    b) Lovin' + Losin' ☐

    c) Breathin' + Believin' ☐

    d) Bustin' + Dronin' ☐

2. The artwork for the front cover of the album is a Graham Coxon oil painting entitled what?

    a) Spectator ☐

    b) Apprentice ☐

    c) Nuance ☐

    d) Lothario ☐

3. Who produced the album?

    a) William Orbit ☐

    b) Orbital ☐

    c) System 7 ☐

    d) Leftfield ☐

4. Released in February 1999 what is the lead single of the album?

   a) No Distance Left to Run ☐

   b) Battle ☐

   c) Tender ☐

   d) Bugman ☐

5. What is searching for Coxon in the "Coffee & TV" music video?

   a) A Sugar Sachet ☐

   b) A Tea Pot ☐

   c) A Coffee Jar ☐

   d) A Milk Carton ☐

6. The final single to be released from the album was "No Distance Left to Run" it is widely understood that it was written after Damon split from whom?

   a) Donna Matthews ☐

   b) Justine Frischmann ☐

   c) Annie Holland ☐

   d) Louise Wener ☐

7. Which album track shares its name with a song
   by Oasis and Tool?

   a) Some Might Say ☐

   b) Underneath the Sky ☐

   c) Swamp Song ☐

   d) Hello ☐

8. In 1999 which UK festival did Blur headline?

   a) Reading Festival ☐

   b) Glastonbury ☐

   c) V Festival ☐

   d) Isle of Wight ☐

9. In December 1999 Blur undertook a short
   tour around the UK - what was the name of
   the tour?

   a) Date Night ☐

   b) Swingers Night ☐

   c) Loners Night ☐

   d) Singles Night ☐

10. After the release of "13" the band released a standalone single to support the bands greatest hits compilation "Blur: The Best Of" what was its title?

    a) Music Is My Radar ☐

    b) The Music is Me ☐

    c) Music Is My Compass ☐

    d) This is the Music ☐

(ANSWERS CAN BE FOUND ON PAGE 83)

Complete the Blur and 13 Lyric

(Five songs from each album)

1. And when she lets me slip away, she turns me on and all my _____ gone

2. I got my head done, when I was _____

3. It's automatic, i need to _____

4. I'm not that good, but I'm not that bad no _____ killer, hooligan guerilla

5. And I feel the light when the sky's just mud and _____

6. Hiding from the _____, waiting for the night to come

7. I've seen so much, I'm going _____ and I'm braindead, virtually

8. Groups using a _____, of another pop group

9. I left my street, I'm a _____, pulling away, in my machine

10. I don't want to see you, 'cause I know the _____ that you keep

(ANSWERS CAN BE FOUND ON PAGE 84)

Dave in Profile

1. What is Dave's middle name?

    a) Spenser de Clause ☐

    b) Alexander de Horne ☐

    c) Pierre de Carlos ☐

    d) Marcus de Huracan ☐

2. What was the title of the South Park-esque animated show that Dave directed in 2005?

    a) Empire State ☐

    b) Russian Square ☐

    c) Empire Square ☐

    d) Russian State ☐

3. What did Dave obtain in 1995?

    a) A Full Pilots Licence ☐

    b) A Master of Art ☐

    c) A Black Belt in Judo ☐

    d) A Shotgun Licence ☐

4. In 2014 which radio station did Dave have a regular Sunday night show?

    a) Radio 1 ☐

    b) Classic FM ☐

    c) Virgin Radio ☐

    d) XFM ☐

5. In 2017 what honorary doctorate did Dave receive from Greenwich University?

    a) Music ☐

    b) Biology ☐

    c) Law ☐

    d) Art ☐

6. Which political party did Dave serve for Norfolk County Council between 2017 and 2021?

    a) Independent ☐

    b) Liberal Democrats ☐

    c) Labour ☐

    d) Conservative ☐

7. In 2018 Dave appeared in a video for which "Slaves" single? He played the role of an auditioning drummer

   a) Follow the Drinking Gourd ☐

   b) Chokehold ☐

   c) Steal Away ☐

   d) Song of the Free ☐

8. In 2021 Dave signed a record deal with which label?

   a) Making Vinyl ☐

   b) Classic Vinyl ☐

   c) Cooking Vinyl ☐

   d) Baking Vinyl ☐

9. What was the title of his first solo single released in July 2022?

   a) London Bridge ☐

   b) Vauxhall Bridge ☐

   c) Tower Bridge ☐

   d) Battersea Bridge ☐

10. And what was the title of his debut album that followed in 2023?

    a) Video Songs ☐

    b) Television Songs ☐

    c) Online Songs ☐

    d) Radio Songs ☐

(ANSWERS CAN BE FOUND ON PAGE 85)

Think Tank Era

1. What is the title of the standalone single that Blur released in advance of "Think Tank"?

    a) Drop the Bomb on Yourself ☐

    b) Don't Bomb When You Are the Bomb ☐

    c) No Bomb is a Good Thing ☐

    d) When the Bomb is Not the Bomb ☐

2. The album cover for "Think Tank" was created by which artist?

    a) Jackson Pollock ☐

    b) Banksy ☐

    c) Frida Kahlo ☐

    d) Ai Weiwei ☐

3. Which member of the band does not feature musically on "Think Tank" due to a spell in rehab and a breakdown in relations?

    a) Damon ☐

    b) Alex ☐

    c) Dave ☐

    d) Graham ☐

4. Simon Tong filled in with the band whilst they were on tour - with which band had he made his name?

    a) The Verve ☐

    b) Supergrass ☐

    c) The Happy Mondays ☐

    d) The Inspiral Carpets ☐

5. What is the title of the opening track on the album?

    a) Ambulance ☐

    b) Brothers and Sisters ☐

    c) Caravan ☐

    d) Sweet Song ☐

6. Alongside Blur who helped to produce "Crazy Beat"?

    a) Nigel Godrich ☐

    b) Mark Ronson ☐

    c) Jack White ☐

    d) Norman Cook ☐

7. What is the title of the lead single from the album?

    a) Good Song ☐

    b) Crazy Beat ☐

    c) Out of Time ☐

    d) Jets ☐

8. In which North African country was part of the album recorded?

    a) Algeria ☐

    b) Egypt ☐

    c) Morocco ☐

    d) Tunisia ☐

9. What number did the album reach in the UK charts?

    a) 1 ☐

    b) 3 ☐

    c) 5 ☐

    d) 10 ☐

10. On which album track does Dave play guitar?

    a) Battery in Your Leg ☐

    b) Out of Time ☐

    c) Gene by Gene ☐

    d) On the Way to the Club ☐

(ANSWERS CAN BE FOUND ON PAGE 86)

The Magic Whip Era

1. What language is "The Magic Whip" written in on the album cover?

   a) Vietnamese ☐

   b) Korean ☐

   c) Japanese ☐

   d) Chinese ☐

2. Written in neon it features alongside which object?

   a) A Warning Sign ☐

   b) An Ice Cream Cone ☐

   c) A Hot Dog ☐

   d) An Exit Sign ☐

3. What is the opening track of the album?

   a) I Broadcast ☐

   b) Ghost Ship ☐

   c) Lonesome Street ☐

   d) New World Towers ☐

4. What is the title of the first single to be released from the album?

    a) There Are Too Many of Us ☐

    b) Lonesome Street ☐

    c) I Broadcast ☐

    d) Go Out ☐

5. While promoting the album Blur performed "Ong Ong" on which US television show?

    a) Jimmy Kimmel Live! ☐

    b) Late Night Show ☐

    c) The Daily Show ☐

    d) The Tonight Show ☐

6. Complete the title of this album track "My Terracotta _____"

    a) Heart ☐

    b) Smile ☐

    c) Love ☐

    d) Frame ☐

7. The album was released by which record label in North America?

    a) Geffen ☐

    b) Warner Bros. ☐

    c) EMI ☐

    d) PDC Records ☐

8. In 2015 Blur played the British Summertime Festival in which London Park?

    a) Green Park ☐

    b) St. James's Park ☐

    c) Battersea Park ☐

    d) Hyde Park ☐

9. In June 2015 Blur performed at a one-off 20th anniversary TV special of which show?

    a) The Tube ☐

    b) The Word ☐

    c) TFI Friday ☐

    d) The Eleven O'clock Show ☐

10. What is the title of the albums closing track?

   a) Thought I Was a Spaceman ☐

   b) Pyongyang ☐

   c) Mirrorball ☐

   d) Ghost Ship ☐

(ANSWERS CAN BE FOUND ON PAGE 87)

SECTION SIXTEEN

Complete the Think Tank and The Magic Whip lyric

(Five songs from each album)

1. I ain't got nothing to be _____ of

2. Feel the sunshine on your face, it's in a _____ now

3. You've got to get it together, stop shooting at me, you're just a _____ industry

4. TVs dead and there ain't no _____ in my head

5. A cartoon in a ketamine, _____ mixed with margarine

6. Step inside the tarmac ride, to the land that
   _____ forgot

7. I get a set alone, dancing with _____

8. I love the aspects of another city; it's got
   your number and your _____ type

9. We all believe in praying, for our
   _____

10. 'Cause the tarmac was melting and the
    people seem to sway in the _____

(ANSWERS CAN BE FOUND ON PAGE 88)

SECTION SEVENTEEN
Damon in Profile

1. In which area of London was Damon born in 1958?

    a) Whitechapel ☐

    b) Hackney ☐

    c) Shoreditch ☐

    d) Brixton ☐

2. What was the name of Damon's first band? They were a synth pop duo

    a) Two in View ☐

    b) A Few is Two ☐

    c) One plus One is Two ☐

    d) Two's a Crowd ☐

3. At the age of six who did Damon see in his first concert?

    a) The Dave Clark Five ☐

    b) The Jacksons ☐

    c) The Osmonds ☐

    d) The Monkees ☐

4. What was the title of the 1997 film that Damon appeared in alongside Ray Winstone and Robert Carlyle?

   a) Face ☐

   b) Safer ☐

   c) Affront ☐

   d) Stranger ☐

5. Who did Damon originally form Gorillaz with?

   a) Gary Hewlett ☐

   b) Gary Humphries ☐

   c) Jamie Humphries ☐

   d) Jamie Hewlett ☐

6. What was the Gorillaz debut single released in March 2001?

   a) Clint Eastwood ☐

   b) 19-2000 ☐

   c) Rock the House ☐

   d) Tomorrow Comes Today ☐

7. The Good, The Bad & the Queen began with Damon working with which producer?

    a) The Chainsmokers ☐

    b) Danger Mouse ☐

    c) Nile Rodgers ☐

    d) Skrillex ☐

8. Paul Simonen would later join the band on bass - with which punk band did he make his name?

    a) The Damned ☐

    b) The Ramones ☐

    c) The Sex Pistols ☐

    d) The Clash ☐

9. What is the title of Damon's debut album released in April 2014?

    a) Everyday Androids ☐

    b) Everyday Animals ☐

    c) Everyday Robots ☐

    d) Everyday People ☐

10. Which country granted Damon citizenship in 2020?

    a) America ☐

    b) The Netherlands ☐

    c) Japan ☐

    d) Iceland ☐

(ANSWERS CAN BE FOUND ON PAGE 89)

The Ballad of Darren Era

1. What features on the front cover of the album?

    a) A Dance Floor ☐

    b) A Supermarket ☐

    c) A Factory ☐

    d) A Swimming Pool ☐

2. What is the title of the lead single from the album?

    a) Barbaric ☐

    b) The Narcissist ☐

    c) The Heights ☐

    d) Goodbye Albert ☐

3. Who produced the album?

    a) Robert Ford ☐

    b) James Lee ☐

    c) James Ford ☐

    d) Robert Lee ☐

4. The title of the album references Darren "Smoggy" Evans - what was his role for the band?

    a) Bodyguard ☐

    b) Roadie ☐

    c) Chef ☐

    d) Driver ☐

5. Which of the following bands supported Blur at one of their 2023 summer Wembley shows?

    a) Idles ☐

    b) Blossoms ☐

    c) Sleaford Mods ☐

    d) The Wombats ☐

6. Which location in Florida features in the title of an album track?

    a) The Everglades ☐

    b) Miami ☐

    c) Fort Lauderdale ☐

    d) Key West ☐

7. Complete the title of this album track "Russian _____"

    a) Dolls ☐

    b) Hearts ☐

    c) Rides ☐

    d) Strings ☐

8. On which bonus album track does Graham take over lead vocals?

    a) Far Away Island ☐

    b) Avalon ☐

    c) Sticks and Stones ☐

    d) March of the Hares ☐

9. Which music magazine voted "The Ballad of Darren" the best album of 2023?

    a) NME ☐

    b) Mojo ☐

    c) Melody Maker ☐

    d) Rolling Stone ☐

10. In 2024 a documentary film was released following the album - what is its title?

    a) In the End ☐

    b) No Way Out ☐

    c) No Way In ☐

    d) To the End ☐

(ANSWERS CAN BE FOUND ON PAGE 90)

Complete the Ballad of Darren Lyric

1. I know I'm already _____ when I look in your eyes

2. 'Cause there's something coming down here and it's livin' under the _____

3. Empty grove, winter darkness, we're taking down the _____, very soon

4. I saw the solstice, the _____ station on the road

5. I'm dancing alone with the moon and the white _____

(ANSWERS CAN BE FOUND ON PAGE 91)

Opening Lyrics Quiz

Simply write the title of the songs that corresponds to the opening lyric – one from each studio album

1. I see her face every day, I see her face, doesn't help me

   _____

2. He's a twentieth century boy, with his hands on the rails

   _____

3. She says there's ants in the carpet, dirty little monsters

   _____

4. The suburbs, they are dreaming, they're a twinkle in her eye

   _____

5. Holy man tiptoes his way across the Ganges

   _____

6. Do you feel like a chainstore? Practically floored

_____

7. Where's the love song to set us free?

_____

8. What do you got? Mass produced in somewhere hot

_____

9. Looked in the mirror, so many people standing there

_____

(ANSWERS CAN BE FOUND ON PAGE 92)

Ten Final Questions

1. When Damon's parents moved to London in the 1960s, they rented a flat in Emperors Gate, Kensington next door to which singer?

    a) John Lennon ☐

    b) Elton John ☐

    c) Rod Stewart ☐

    d) Freddie Mercury ☐

2. Which Rod Stewart song did the band cover for a 1992 NME covers album?

    a) Maggie May ☐

    b) Some Guys Have All the Luck ☐

    c) Rhythm of My Heart ☐

    d) The First Cut is the Deepest ☐

3. What is the title of the 1993 fly on the wall documentary about the band?

    a) Starryeyes ☐

    b) Starless ☐

    c) Starshaped ☐

    d) Starcrossed ☐

4. Which duo remixed "Girls & Boys" in 1994?

    a) Chemical Brothers ☐

    b) The Pet Shop Boys ☐

    c) Daft Punk ☐

    d) Underworld ☐

5. Which Blur song features on the soundtrack to 1998 film "Dead Man on Campus"?

    a) Sheriff Song ☐

    b) Police Song ☐

    c) Soldier Song ☐

    d) Cowboy Song ☐

6. What was the title of the 2003 E.P release featuring demos by Damon?

    a) Demoneyes ☐

    b) Demograffic ☐

    c) Demonstraight ☐

    d) Democrazy ☐

7. Of the nine Blur studio albums how many have reached number one in the UK charts?

    a) Three ☐

    b) Five ☐

    c) Seven ☐

    d) Eight ☐

8. What was the title of the 7" single released in 2010 for Record Store Day?

    a) Good Days ☐

    b) Fool's Day ☐

    c) Same Day ☐

    d) Strange Days ☐

9. In 2013 Damon and Graham joined Paul Weller and Noel Gallagher to perform which Blur song at the Teenage Cancer Trust charity event?

    a) Coffee & TV ☐

    b) This is a Low ☐

    c) Tender ☐

    d) Song 2 ☐

10. In 2013 which festival were Blur due to play?
The entire festival was cancelled for unknown
reasons

   a) Tokyo Rocks ☐

   b) Lollapalooza ☐

   c) Desert Festival ☐

   d) Fire Festival ☐

(ANSWERS CAN BE FOUND ON PAGE 93)

ANSWERS

Section One: Early Days

1. d) Saxophone ☐
2. c) Circus ☐
3. d) Seymour ☐
4. c) Goldsmiths ☐
5. d) East Anglian Railway ☐
6. b) Food Records ☐
7. a) Brixton Academy ☐
8. c) The Cramps ☐
9. b) Eggs 'n' Baker ☐
10. c) Rotterdam ☐

/10

Section Two: Leisure Era

1. c) She's So High ☐
2. d) Bathing Hat ☐
3. b) 7 ☐
4. a) Sing ☐
5. d) Kurt Cobain ☐
6. b) A Worm ☐
7. a) Scrabble ☐
8. a) Down ☐
9. a) Stephen Street ☐
10. c) Popscene ☐

/10

Section Three: Modern Life is Rubbish Era

1. b) Rollercoaster Tour ☐
2. c) Butch Vig ☐
3. d) Britain Vs America ☐
4. a) A Steam Train ☐
5. d) For Tomorrow ☐
6. b) Julian ☐
7. d) SBK ☐
8. c) Maggie May ☐
9. a) A Burger ☐
10. d) Substitute ☐

/10

Section Four: Leisure and Modern Life is Rubbish Lyrics

1. Crawl ☐
2. Rumble ☐
3. Love ☐
4. Think ☐
5. Forgive ☐
6. Westway ☐
7. Collar ☐
8. Landlord ☐
9. England ☐
10. Breathing ☐

/10

Section Five: Alex in Profile

1. c) Steven Alexander James ☐
2. d) Bournemouth ☐
3. c) Chickenpox ☐
4. b) Fat Les ☐
5. a) Cheese Farm ☐
6. a) Read My Lips ☐
7. c) Claire ☐
8. d) Five ☐
9. c) Alex James's Date Night ☐
10. d) The Big Feastival ☐

/10

Section Six: Parklife Era

1. b) Girls & Boys ☐
2. a) Maison Rouge ☐
3. a) Greyhounds ☐
4. d) London ☐
5. c) Phil Daniels ☐
6. a) Far Out ☐
7. c) Stereolab ☐
8. d) Alexandra Palace ☐
9. b) Debt ☐
10. a) This Is a Low ☐

/10

Section Seven: The Great Escape Era

1. d) Roll with It ☐
2. a) Damien Hirst ☐
3. c) Cars ☐
4. b) Ken Livingstone ☐
5. d) A Clockwork Orange ☐
6. a) Dublin Castle ☐
7. d) Speedboat ☐
8. b) Quango ☐
9. b) Charmless Man ☐
10. c) Yuko and Hiro ☐

/10

Section Eight: Parklife and The Great Escape Lyrics

1. Blisters ☐
2. Thirty ☐
3. Wednesdays ☐
4. Dumb ☐
5. Thames ☐
6. Lingerie ☐
7. Prozac ☐
8. Cavalry ☐
9. Satellites ☐
10. Families ☐

/10

Section Nine: Graham In Profile

1. b) Graham Leslie Coxon ☐
2. c) Rinteln, Germany ☐
3. d) Derby County ☐
4. a) Blue Peter ☐
5. d) Fine Arts ☐
6. a) The Sky is Too High ☐
7. c) Syd Barrett ☐
8. b) Zodiac ☐
9. d) Peter Doherty ☐
10. c) Verse, Chorus, Monster! ☐

/10

Section Ten: Blur (Album) Era

1. d) A Hospital ☐
2. b) Reykjavik ☐
3. d) You're So Great ☐
4. b) Beetlebum ☐
5. d) Song 2 ☐
6. b) Bombs ☐
7. c) M.O.R ☐
8. d) The Beach ☐
9. a) Japan ☐
10. a) Essex Dogs ☐

/10

Section Eleven: 13 Era

1. d) Bustin' + Dronin' ☐
2. b) Apprentice ☐
3. a) William Orbit ☐
4. c) Tender ☐
5. d) A Milk Carton ☐
6. b) Justine Frischmann ☐
7. c) Swamp Song ☐
8. a) Reading Festival ☐
9. d) Singles Night ☐
10. a) Music Is My Radar ☐

/10

Section Twelve: Blur and 13 lyrics

1. Violence ☐
2. Young ☐
3. Unload ☐
4. Psycho ☐
5. Grey ☐
6. Sun ☐
7. Blind ☐
8. Loop ☐
9. Guillotine ☐
10. Dreams ☐

/10

Section Thirteen: Dave in Profile

1. b) Alexander de Horne ☐
2. c) Empire Square ☐
3. a) A Full Pilots Licence ☐
4. d) XFM ☐
5. c) Law ☐
6. c) Labour ☐
7. b) Chokehold ☐
8. c) Cooking Vinyl ☐
9. a) London Bridge ☐
10. d) Radio Songs ☐

/10

Section Fourteen: Think Tank Era

1. b) Don't Bomb When You Are the Bomb ☐
2. b) Banksy ☐
3. d) Graham ☐
4. a) The Verve ☐
5. a) Ambulance ☐
6. d) Norman Cook ☐
7. c) Out of Time ☐
8. c) Morocco ☐
9. a) 1 ☐
10. d) On the Way to the Club ☐

/10

Section Fifteen: The Magic Whip Era

1. d) Chinese ☐
2. b) An Ice Cream Cone ☐
3. c) Lonesome Street ☐
4. d) Go Out ☐
5. d) The Tonight Show ☐
6. a) Heart ☐
7. b) Warner Bros. ☐
8. d) Hyde Park ☐
9. c) TFI Friday ☐
10. c) Mirrorball ☐

/10

Section Sixteen: Think Tank and The Magic Whip Lyrics

1. Scared ☐
2. Computer ☐
3. Teenage ☐
4. War ☐
5. Jelly ☐
6. Crime ☐
7. Myself ☐
8. Blood ☐
9. Immortality ☐
10. Underground ☐

/10

Section Seventeen: Damon in Profile

1. a) Whitechapel ☐
2. d) Two's a Crowd ☐
3. c) The Osmonds ☐
4. a) Face ☐
5. d) Jamie Hewlett ☐
6. a) Clint Eastwood ☐
7. b) Danger Mouse ☐
8. d) The Clash ☐
9. c) Everyday Robots ☐
10. d) Iceland ☐

/10

Section Eighteen: The Ballad of Darren Era

1. d) A swimming pool ☐
2. b) The Narcissist ☐
3. c) James Ford ☐
4. a) Bodyguard ☐
5. c) Sleaford Mods ☐
6. a) The Everglades ☐
7. d) Strings ☐
8. c) Sticks and Stones ☐
9. b) Mojo ☐
10. d) To the End ☐

/10

Section Nineteen: The Ballad of Darren Lyrics

1. Breaking ☐
2. Floorboards ☐
3. Scaffolds ☐
4. Service ☐
5. Whale ☐

/5

Section Twenty: Opening Lyric Quiz

1. She's So High
2. For Tomorrow
3. End of a Century
4. Stereotypes
5. On Your Own
6. Coffee & TV
7. Out of Time
8. Lonesome Street
9. The Narcissist

/9

Section Twenty-One: Ten Final Questions

1. a) John Lennon ☐
2. a) Maggie May ☐
3. c) Starshaped ☐
4. b) The Pet Shop Boys ☐
5. d) Cowboy Song ☐
6. d) Democrazy ☐
7. c) Seven ☐
8. b) Fool's Day ☐
9. c) Tender ☐
10. a) Tokyo Rocks ☐

/10

That completes the quiz and with a total of 204 points available – where do you stand?

175-204 Brit Pop Legend

150-174 You're so Great

125-149 This is a High!

100-124 Room for Improvement

51-99 Still learning the ropes.

0-50 All still a Blur

Hopefully you have enjoyed this little quiz book and it has been a challenge but your knowledge has extended and been rewarded. Now it's time to challenge your friends and family.

Take away multiple choice options for the easier questions and use the book to teach the next generation of fans about the history of this great band.

Printed in Dunstable, United Kingdom